To each and every EXPERT—to those parents, grandparents, teachers, librarians, caregivers, child development specialists, pediatricians, obstetricians, nurses, child psychologists, psychoanalysts, health educators, and clergy who read over and looked over our work, talked to us, taught us, and corrected us over and over again as we created this book for young children. We could not have created this book without you. THANK YOU!—R. H. H.

For Eva and her parents, Jenn and Fred

N. B. W.

Text copyright © 2013 by Bee Productions, Inc.
Illustrations copyright © 2013 by Nadine Bernard Westcott

First edition 2013

Library of Congress Cataloging-in-Publication Data

Harris, Robie H.
What's in there? : All about before you were born / Robie H. Harris; illustrated by Nadine Bernard Westcott.—1st ed.
p. cm.
ISBN 978-0-7636-3630-2
1. Human reproduction—Juvenile literature. 2. Childbirth—Juvenile literature.
3. Sex instruction for children—Juvenile literature. I. Westcott, Nadine Bernard, ill. II. Title. III. Series.
QP251.5.H369 2010
612.6—dc22   2008025455

22 23 TLF 10 9 8 7 6 5 4

Printed in Dongguan, Guangdong, China

This book was typeset in Berkeley Old Style.
The illustrations were created digitally.

Candlewick Press
99 Dover Street
Somerville, Massachusetts 02144

visit us at www.candlewick.com

What's In There?

All About Before You Were Born

Robie H. Harris

illustrated by Nadine Bernard Westcott

CANDLEWICK PRESS

New babies begin to grow in a special place inside a woman's body called the uterus. That's where you grew before you were born. That's where everybody grew before they were born.

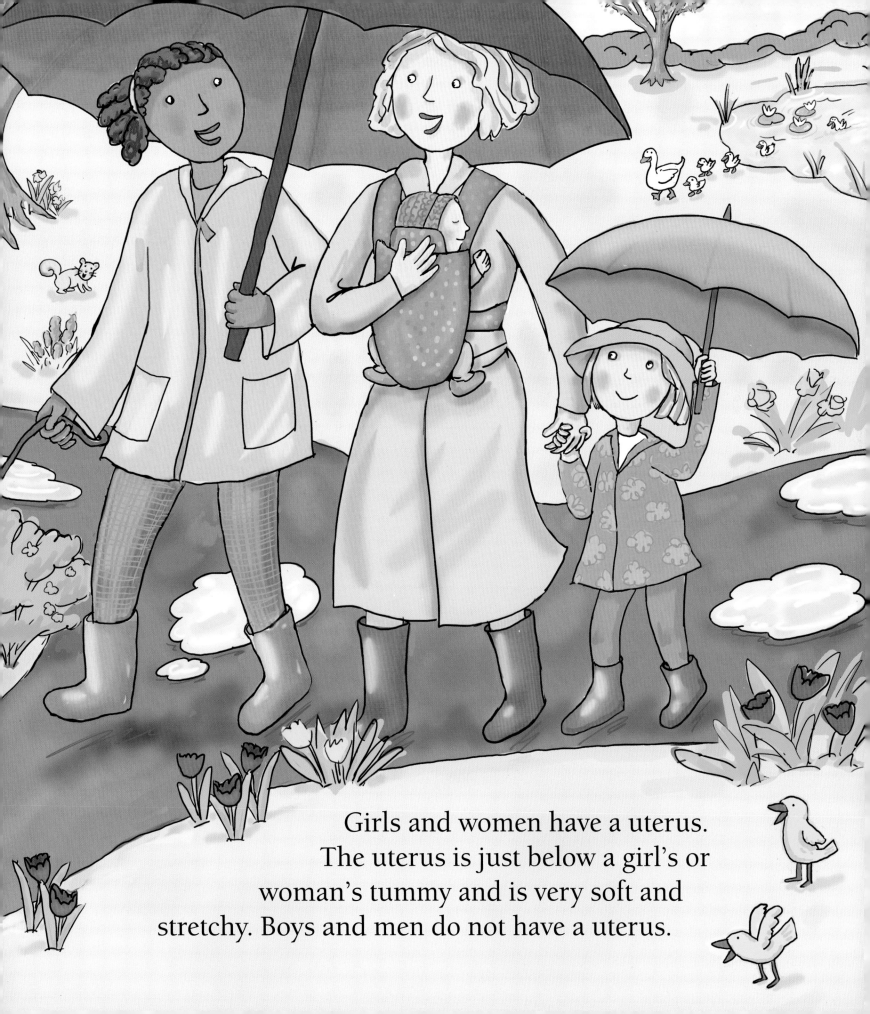

Girls and women have a uterus.
The uterus is just below a girl's or
woman's tummy and is very soft and
stretchy. Boys and men do not have a uterus.

All growing babies begin as one tiny cell. Half of this cell comes from a woman's body. The other half comes from a man's body. Together, they can grow into a baby.

When a growing baby is inside the uterus and is only a few days old, it has already grown into a ball of cells. That ball is the size of the teeniest, tiniest dot—about the size of a pencil dot.

Soon, the growing baby is about the size of an apple seed. Its backbone has started to grow. And its heart has started to beat. It has a tiny tail and looks a lot like a tadpole.

The whole time a growing baby is inside a woman's uterus, it floats in warm water. The water all around the growing baby keeps it warm and safe from bumps and pokes.

Then the growing baby grows even more. Soon, it is about the size of a big peach.

Now it has eyes, ears, lips, arms, fingers, legs, toes—and a nose. Its bones and muscles are growing. Its tail has begun to disappear, and it is beginning to look more like a baby.

Now the growing baby has the special part that will make it a girl or a boy—a vagina for a girl and a penis for a boy. Soft, fuzzy hair covers its whole body! And its fingernails and toenails have started to grow.

When a growing baby is inside a woman's uterus, food and drinks and air go into her body. The food goes into the woman's tummy, where it breaks into very, very tiny bits of food.

Then those tiny bits of food and the drinks and air pass through a special twisty tube right into the growing baby's body—and help the baby to stay healthy and to grow bigger and stronger.

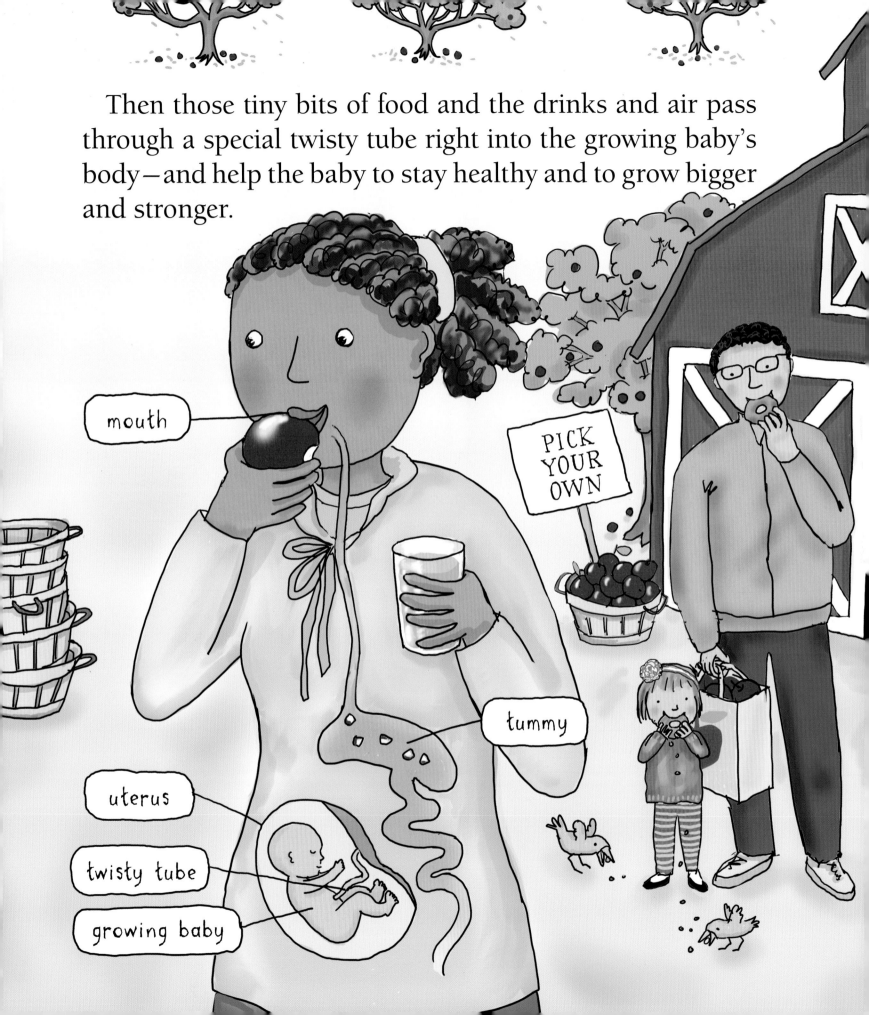

mouth

PICK YOUR OWN

tummy

uterus

twisty tube

growing baby

Soon, the growing baby is about the size of a small pumpkin. Now it can hear noises, like when a doorbell rings *ding-dong!* or a person sings "La-la-la-laaaaa!" And it can make noises—even hiccups and burps.

It can also see light. And it can kick, punch, and somersault.

Now the growing baby's lungs are pushing in and out. It's practicing how to breathe. And it's growing eyebrows and eyelashes and hair on its head. It can open and close its eyes. It can suck its thumb and sleep.

To make more room for the growing baby, the woman's uterus and skin stretch and grow bigger—the same way a balloon stretches and grows bigger.

Sometimes, the baby drinks the water it floats in and pees a little bit. But most growing babies do not poop inside the uterus.

After growing for a very long time—nine whole months—the growing baby is about the size of a watermelon.

Now its tummy, brain, and heart—and all the other parts of its body—are working very, very well. And it's big enough, and strong enough, and ready to be born.

When a new baby is ready to be born, its mommy's muscles squeeze and push the baby out of her uterus.

Soon the baby comes out through a stretchy opening between its mommy's legs called the vagina. And the baby is born! Most babies let out a cry the moment they are born.

Sometimes, the doctor makes a special cut into the mommy's uterus and lifts the baby out. And the baby is born! Then the mommy's cut is sewn up with a special thread. The cutting and sewing does not hurt the mommy or the baby.

As soon as the baby is born, the doctor cuts the twisty tube. This cutting does not hurt the baby or the mommy.

Your bellybutton is where the twisty tube was attached to you when you were growing inside the uterus.

A few moments later, the baby is wiped off, dressed in a diaper, undershirt, and hat, and wrapped in a warm, soft, cozy blanket.

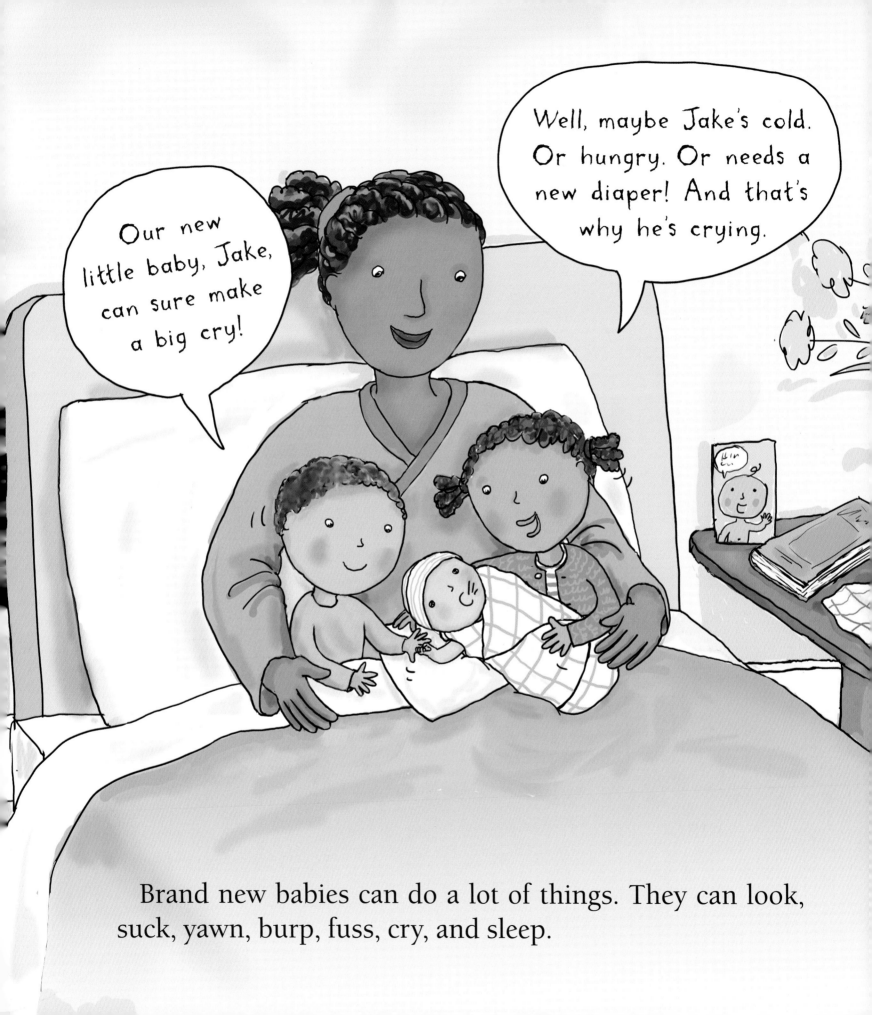

Brand new babies can do a lot of things. They can look, suck, yawn, burp, fuss, cry, and sleep.

Cuddling, holding, kissing, and even looking at a new baby feels so wonderful. So does whispering, talking, or singing to a new baby.

Saying, "I love you!" to a baby feels wonderful too.

Sometimes when babies are born, two or even more babies come out. These two babies are called twins. Some twins are two girls. Some are two boys. Some are a girl and a boy.

When three babies come out, they are called triplets. And sometimes—but not very often—when babies are born, four or five or six babies come out.

But our gerbil babies were a whole lot tinier than our new baby, Jake.

All babies are born into or adopted into their family. And the day a baby is born is that baby's birthday. Every baby's birthday, and child's birthday, and grown-up's birthday is a very, very special day.

Everybody was a baby once. Even you!

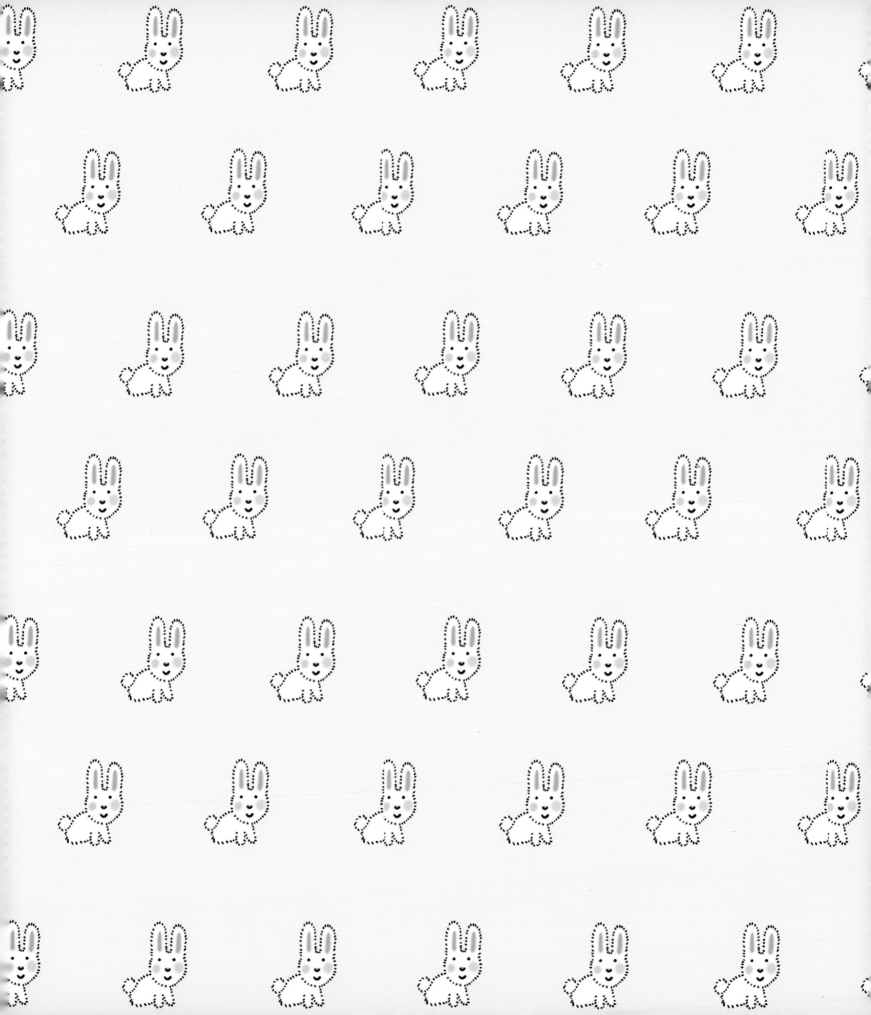